County Derry

Table of Contents

Introduction   5

County Derry - population, name, name in Irish,   7
nickname, maint towns and cities

Bordering Counties   14

Crest - symbols and colors meanings   16

Natural Features -rivers, lakes, mountains   18

Place of Interest   21

Famous People   23

Sports Teams   24

Introduction

Hello everyone, my name is Alex Tudor and I am excited to share my project on County Derry with you.

I am 11 years old and currently in grade 4 at St. Francis' National School in Newcastle, Co. Wicklow.

County Derry, also known as County Londonderry, is a county located in Northern Ireland with a rich history and culture. Throughout this project, I will be exploring the many fascinating aspects of County Derry, including its geography, history, and notable landmarks.

So come along on this journey with me and let's discover all that County Derry has to offer!

County Derry

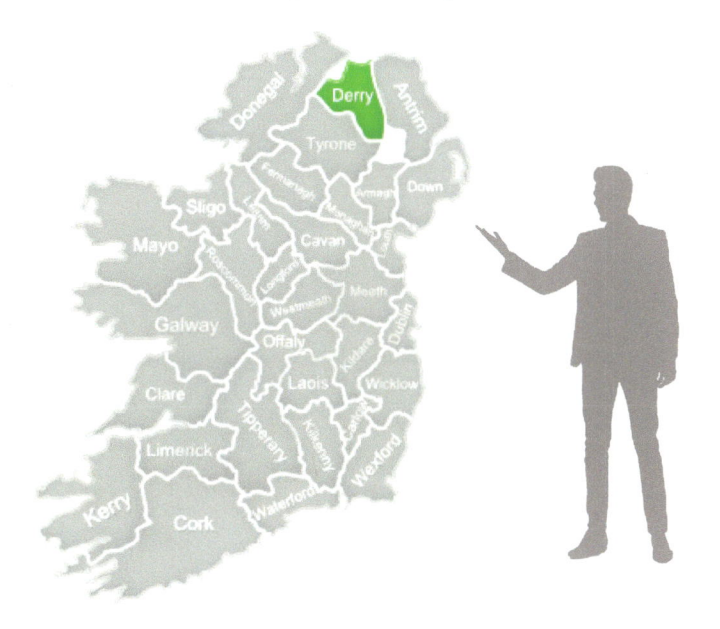

County Londonderry, also known as County Derry, is one of the six counties of Northern Ireland, one of the thirty two counties of Ireland and one of the nine counties of Ulster. Before the partition of Ireland, it was one of the counties of the Kingdom of Ireland from 1613 onward and then of the United Kingdom after the Acts of Union 1800. Adjoining the north-west shore of Lough Neagh, the county covers an area of 2,118 km2 and today has a population of about 247,132 and is known for its stunning coastline, rich history, and vibrant culture.

DID YOU KNOW

Several movies and TV shows have been filmed in County Derry, including the TV series "Derry Girls".

County Derry

The place name **Derry** is an anglicisation of the Old Irish Daire (Modern Irish Doire), meaning "oak-grove" or "oak-wood".

St Colmcille first named the area when he set up a monastry in an Oak grove at the site, calling it "Doire Colmcille" ("Colmcille's Oak Grove"). When English settlers arrived much later they founded a city near the ruins of the monastry and named it "London Doire", using part of the local name and the name of their own home town. This is anglicised as "Londonderry". When the counties were set up, county Londonderry was named after the city. Today the anglicised version of Doire ("Derry") is often used as an abbreviation.

Riverfront and Walled City masterplan, Derry

Derry City Walls

> Derry City is the fourth-largest city in Northern Ireland.

The largest city in County Derry is **Derry**, also known as Londonderry, which is located on the banks of the River Foyle. Derry is a vibrant and cosmopolitan city with a rich history and a strong cultural identity.

Derry also boasts a number of excellent visitor attractions. The **Tower Museum** is an award winning attraction, telling the history of the city and includes a range of exhibitions, while Derry's **Guildhall, St Columb's Cathedral, St Eugene's Cathedral and St Augustine's Chapel** are all historic buildings of stunning architecture.

Other sights include the fascinating **Bogside Murals** found on the walls of what is known as Free Derry Corner and depict various events in the history of the town. A more contemporary sculpture in the city, known as **Hands Across the Divide.**

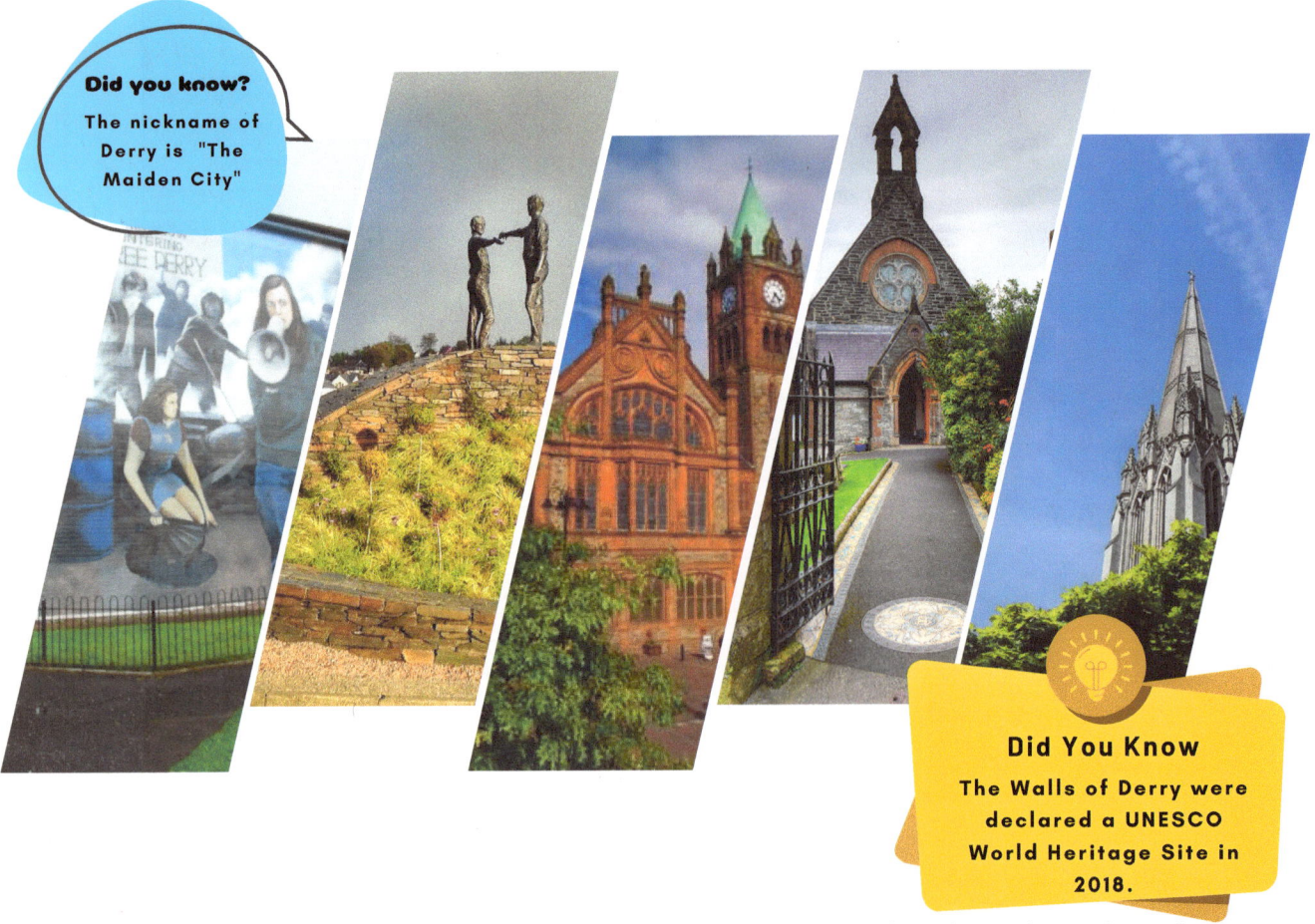

> **Did you know?**
> The nickname of Derry is "The Maiden City"

> **Did You Know**
> The Walls of Derry were declared a UNESCO World Heritage Site in 2018.

The city walls are the best-preserved in all of Ireland and make about a one-mile circumference around the city centre.

The walls, which date back to the 17th century, and which are the only completely intact city walls in Ireland. The presence of the walls earned Derry the nickname, "The Maiden City", for their defences were never breached, even during the 1689 Siege of Derry.

Tower Museum

DID YOU KNOW ?

Many famous people have visited County Derry over the years. Some notable visitors include former U.S. President Bill Clinton, who visited Derry in 1995 and spoke at a peace rally in the city, and the actor Liam Neeson, who was born in Ballymena in County Antrim but grew up in Ballymena in County Derry.

Another important town in County Derry is **Coleraine**, which is situated on the River Bann. Coleraine is a bustling market town with a rich history and a range of cultural attractions, including the Riverside Theatre and the Bann Valley Heritage Centre. The town is also a popular destination for shoppers, with a range of high-street stores and independent boutiques.

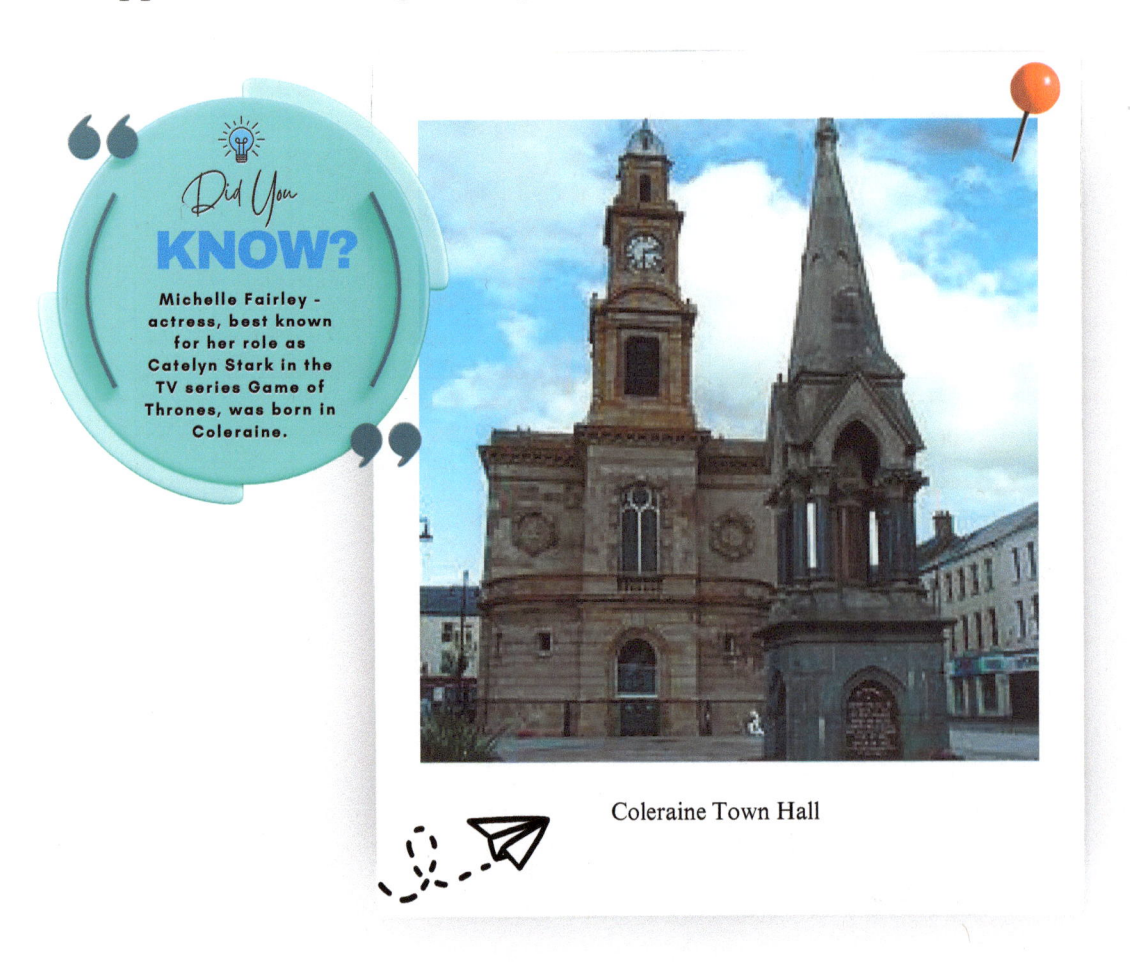

> **Did You KNOW?**
> Michelle Fairley - actress, best known for her role as Catelyn Stark in the TV series Game of Thrones, was born in Coleraine.

Coleraine Town Hall

Limavady is another town in County Derry that is well worth a visit. Located on the banks of the River Roe, Limavady is a small, picturesque town with a rich history and a strong cultural identity. The town is known for its stunning countryside and its range of outdoor activities, including hiking, cycling, and fishing.

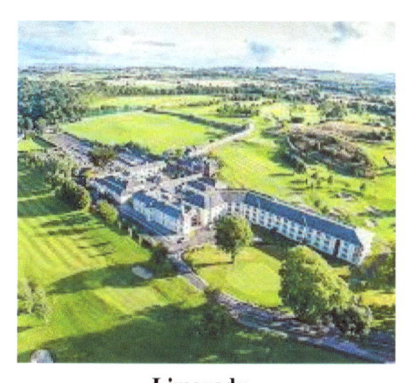

Limavady **Magherafelt** **Portstewart**

Other important towns and villages in County Derry include **Magherafelt**, a market town with a strong agricultural heritage.

Portstewart, a popular seaside resort with a beautiful beach and stunning views over the Atlantic.

And **Castledawson**, a picturesque village located on the banks of the River Moyola.

DID YOU KNOW

Some scenes from TV series "Game of Thrones" were filmed in County Derry.

Bordering Counties

Derry is a county in Northern Ireland, situated in the northwest of the country. It is bordered by several other counties, each with its own unique history and culture.

To the east of County Derry is **County Antrim**, which is known for its stunning coastline and the Giant's Causeway, a UNESCO World Heritage site. County Antrim is also home to Belfast, the capital city of Northern Ireland.

To the south of County Derry is **County Tyrone**, which is known for its beautiful countryside and traditional Irish music. County Tyrone is home to the Sperrin Mountains, a range of hills that offer stunning views of the surrounding countryside.

County Antrim   County Tyrone   County Donegal   Atlantic Ocean

To the west of County Derry is **County Donegal**, which is located in the Republic of Ireland. County Donegal is known for its rugged coastline, pristine beaches, and stunning natural beauty. It is also home to the Slieve League Cliffs, which are some of the highest sea cliffs in Europe.

Finally, to the north of County Derry is the **Atlantic Ocean**, which provides the county with stunning views and access to a variety of water-based activities, such as fishing, surfing, and sailing.

DID YOU KNOW?

The Wild Ireland wildlife park near Burnfoot showcases some of Donegal's historic animal species that were hunted to extinction, including brown bears, lynxes and gray wolves.

Overall, the neighbouring counties of County Derry offer a diverse range of attractions and activities, from vibrant cities and stunning landscapes to rich cultural traditions and outdoor adventures.

Crest

The crest of County Derry features three distinct symbols: a red hand, a white flax flower, and the sheafs of wheat. Each of these symbols holds great significance to the history and identity of the county.

The red hand is perhaps the most recognizable symbol on the crest. It is a hand with the fingers pointing upward, all colored red. This is an ancient symbol known as the "Red Hand of Ulster," which has been used for centuries as a symbol of the province of Ulster.

According to legend, the symbol represents the hand of a warrior who cut off his own hand and threw it ashore to claim the land on behalf of his clan. The Red Hand of Ulster has come to represent loyalty, strength, and courage, and it remains a powerful symbol of identity for the people of County Derry.

The white flax flower on the crest represents the long history of flax cultivation in the county. Flax was once a major industry in County Derry, and the county was known for producing some of the finest linen in the world.

The sheafs of wheat on the crest represents the agricultural heritage of County Derry. The county has a long history of farming, and wheat has been a staple crop for centuries. The sheaf of wheat on the crest represents the abundance and fertility of the county's land, as well as the hard work and dedication of the farmers who have cultivated it.

The colors on the crest are also significant. The flax flower is white, which represents innocence and purity.

The wheat sheaf is gold, which represents wealth and prosperity. Together, these colors represent the hopes and aspirations of the people of County Derry.

Natural Features

The county is characterized by its diverse landscape, which includes mountains, lakes, and rivers.

The Sperrin Mountains, which run through the southern part of the county, are the largest range in Northern Ireland, and offer some of the most stunning views in the country. The highest peak in the range is Sawel Mountain.

Sawel Mountain reaches a height of 678 meters.

Sawel Mountain

In addition to the Sperrin Mountains, County Derry is also home to several other noteworthy mountain ranges, including the Binevenagh Range, the Slieve Gallion Range and Donald's Hill, which is the site of an annual car race. These mountains provide ample opportunities for hiking, climbing, and other outdoor activities.

County Derry is home to several rivers, the most significant of which is the River Foyle, which is the fourth-longest river in Ireland. It flows for approximately 129 kilometers through the county, and its estuary forms the natural boundary between Northern Ireland and the Republic of Ireland. Other notable rivers in County Derry include the River Roe, the River Faughan, and the River Bann, which marks the eastern border of the county.

River Foyle

River Faughan

River Ban

Lough Neagh, is the largest lake in Ireland

County Derry is also home to several lakes, both natural and man-made. One of the largest natural lakes in the county is Lough Foyle, which is an estuary fed by the River Foyle. It is an important site for birdlife and has been designated a Special Protection Area (SPA). Other notable lakes in County Derry include Lough Neagh, and Lough Beg, which is a freshwater lough situated in the northwest of the county.

DID YOU KNOW?
"The world is a book, and those who do not travel read only a page."
Saint Augustine

Place of interest

County Derry, also known as County Londonderry, is a beautiful region located in Northern Ireland. There are plenty of tourist attractions in County Derry that are worth visiting. Here are some of the top places to visit:

Mussenden Temple: A striking neoclassical building perched atop a 120ft cliff overlooking the Atlantic Ocean, it offers breathtaking views.

City Walls of Derry: Built in the 17th century, the city walls of Derry are one of the best preserved examples of a walled city in Europe.

Guildhall: A stunning example of neo-gothic architecture, the Guildhall is located in the heart of Derry and is home to a range of exhibitions.

Roe Valley Country Park: Located just outside Limavady, Roe Valley is a beautiful park with forest walks, waterfalls, and a variety of wildlife.

Portstewart Strand: A stunning Blue Flag beach with miles of golden sand and stunning views.

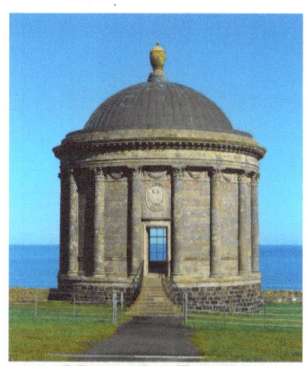

Mussenden Temple

Guildhall

Roe Valley Country Park

The People's Gallery: Also known as the Bogside Murals, this collection of political murals depicts the history of the Troubles in Derry.

Bellaghy Bawn: A well-preserved example of an early 17th-century fortified house located in the village of Bellaghy.

Springhill House: A beautiful 17th-century plantation house with stunning gardens and woodland walks.

Beaghmore Stone Circles: A fascinating prehistoric site consisting of seven stone circles, located in the Sperrin Mountains.

These are just a few of the many wonderful tourist attractions in County Derry. There is plenty to see and do in this beautiful region of Northern Ireland.

DID YOU KNOW

France is the world's most visited country with over 89 million visitors in 2019.

Beaghmore Stone Circles

Famous People

County Derry is home to many famous people from various fields, including music, sports, literature, and politics. Here are some notable individuals from County Derry:

Seamus Heaney - He was an Irish poet, playwright, translator, and lecturer. He was awarded the Nobel Prize in Literature in 1995. He was born in Mossbawn, County Derry.

Brian Friel - He was a playwright, short story writer, and founder of the Field Day Theatre Company. He was born in Omagh, County Tyrone, but spent much of his life in County Derry.

Van Morrison is an Irish singer-songwriter, instrumentalist, and record producer. He is known for various enduring hits including "Brown Eyed Girl" and "Crazy Love". He has experimented with many genres through the years including rock, R&B, folk, blues, and even gospel.

Nadine Coyle is a singer, actress, and model who shot to fame as part of the band Girls Aloud.

Phil Coulter - He is a musician, songwriter, and record producer. He has written many popular songs and has worked with artists such as Van Morrison and Elvis Presley.

ATTENTION!

IMPORTANT:

"The future belongs to those who believe in the beauty of their dreams."
Eleanor Roosevelt

Sports Teams

The county is home to a number of sports teams and events, with Gaelic football and hurling being particularly popular.

Gaelic Football:

The Derry senior football team represents the county in Gaelic football and competes in the All-Ireland Senior Football Championship. They have won the championship three times, with their most recent victory coming in 1993. The county also has a strong tradition of club football, with teams such as Slaughtneil, Ballinderry Shamrocks, and Glenullin among the most successful.

Slaughtneil Team

Hurling:

Derry also has a strong tradition of hurling, with the county's senior hurling team competing in the Christy Ring Cup, which is the second tier of inter-county hurling. The county's most successful hurling club is Kevin Lynch's GAC, which has won numerous county and Ulster titles.

Soccer:

Derry City FC is the only professional soccer team in the county, and they compete in the League of Ireland Premier Division. The club has a strong fan base and has won numerous domestic and international honors, including the League of Ireland title and the FAI Cup.

Rugby:

Rugby is also played in the county, with teams such as City of Derry Rugby Football Club and Limavady Rugby Football Club competing in various leagues and competitions.

Other popular sports in County Derry include basketball, boxing, cricket, and golf, with numerous clubs and facilities available for each sport.

Ingram Content Group UK Ltd.
Milton Keynes UK
UKHW050426010623
422640UK00001B/1